WHEN ABRAHAM
TALKED TO THE TREES

For Donnie, Charlie, and Emma Kate Van Steenwyk. — E. A. V.

For my wife, Deborah, and my daughters, Allison and Caitlin. — B. F.

Text © 2000 by Elizabeth Van Steenwyk
Illustrations © 2000 by Bill Farnsworth
Published 2000 by Eerdmans Books for Young Readers
An imprint of Wm. B. Eerdmans Publishing Company
255 Jefferson S.E., Grand Rapids, Michigan 49503
P.O. Box 163, Cambridge CB3 9PU U.K.

Printed in Hong Kong
02 03 04 05 06   7 6 5 4 3 2
Library of Congress Cataloging-in-Publication Data
Van Steenwyk, Elizabeth.
When Abraham talked to the trees / written by Elizabeth Van Steenwyk:
illustrated by Bill Farnsworth.
p. cm.
ISBN 0-8028-5191-6 (alk.paper)
ISBN 0-8028-5233-5 (pbk : alk.paper)
1. Lincoln, Abraham, 1809-1865—childhood and youth Juvenile literature.
2. Lincoln, Abraham, 1809-1865—Books and reading Juvenile literature.
3. Lincoln, Abraham, 1809-1865—Oratory Juvenile literature.
4. Presidents—United States Biography Juvenile literature.
I. Farnsworth, Bill. II. Title.
E457.32.V27 1999
973.7'092—dc21
(B)   99-39908
CIP
The illustrations were painted in oils on linen.
The text type was set in Goudy Old Style.
The book was designed by Gayle Brown.

WHEN ABRAHAM
TALKED TO THE TREES

Written by
Elizabeth Van Steenwyk

Illustrated by
Bill Farnsworth

Eerdmans Books for Young Readers
Grand Rapids, Michigan   Cambridge, U. K.

When Abraham Lincoln's ma died, she left him a book and the wish to read it every day. The words were hard to figure sometimes, but he tried again and again when chores were finished and the quiet had come.

A year later, Abraham's pa brought a new ma home to Indiana, and a brother and two sisters besides. The new ma had books too, and Abraham liked them best of all.

But there were logs to be split, corn to be hoed, and June berries to be picked. Reading took last place in Abraham's day, but it was always first place in his heart.

Long after sister Sarah and the other children had climbed up to sleep under the roof, Abraham lingered by the firelight. He pondered the words in a book by Aesop, putting them to mind until he could say them without the book.

He recited them to his family. His new ma and old pa and the rest listened as if the words were gospel.

But cousin Dennis had other ideas. "That book's full of lies," he said.

"Mighty fine lies," Abraham replied, and he kept on telling. He had a craving for saying the words aloud.

Wherever he was — helping his pa stump the field or alone in the woods picking sassafras roots and chewing on October grapes — the words of the night previous hovered nearby. He savored them as he did the taste of the sassafras and the balm of the afternoon sun.

Abraham hungered for more learning, but school was a sometime thing. So he read his new ma's book that explained the meanings of words according to a man named Webster. And he read his old ma's Bible each day too. It nourished and filled him as much as the vittles on the table.

Still, he yearned for more.

The two sets of children had mixed together like mush and
molasses in a bowl, and they played easily with one another
in the clearing by the cabin. They rolled hoops made of
hickory saplings and jumped ropes made of grapevines.
Then they played hare and hounds and wet and dry stones.
Finally, when twilight came, they gathered in a fence corner
and listened while Abraham told stories.

Abraham tried his hand at writing words too. Since his family had no paper for foolishness, he wrote on a shovel with ashes or outside in the dirt or snow. When the wind blew or the thaw came, the words disappeared. But there was a place inside him where he stored all the words up against a future day.

Abraham grew in other ways as well.

One day, as he helped his pa build a rail fence they hoped would be higher than a horse, stronger than a bull, and tougher than a goat, two men stopped by.

"Got yourself a mighty big helper, Thomas," one man said to Abraham's pa. "Must be fixing to wade in a deep creek when he's all grown up."

Then the men asked Thomas if he would take charge of building a church just a hoot and a holler away. Everyone said he was best around these parts with a hammer and a saw. And he had the best help — that was plain to see.

Abraham obliged his pa alongside a passel of other men as the church took shape against the sky.

"The trees of the Lord are full of sap," one man offered, noting their sweat as they worked.

Soon, the church filled a place in the woods where the creek took a meander down the hill. Before long, a preacher came. He was bursting with the spirit and made a great commotion each Sunday. He punched the air with his fists and pointed his finger so folks would know the direction of salvation.

It came to Abraham then that there was more to talking than talking. As he filled his pockets with shagbark nuts on the way home from the preaching, he rummaged through the words in his head.

Later, his voice rang in the woods as he practiced aloud. His voice was changing with the rest of him. Sometimes he sounded like a rusty nail on a gate banging shut. Other times he croaked like a bullfrog at twilight. Didn't matter. It was the meaning that counted, not the sound.

At last the time came to try out his newly found notion.

Abraham gathered his mixed-together family around him before he stepped on a stump in the clearing beside the cabin. Other folks came too. Then he repeated the sermons he'd heard, word for word. Again and again and again.

Till nobody was left but the trees.

It didn't matter much to Abraham. Might come a time when other folks would stay and listen to what he had read and written and wanted to say. He would be ready for that day.

When he became President of the United States in 1861, other folks did listen, and listen — and listen some more.

Folks are still listening to this day.